The J. Paul Getty Museum

MUSEUMS OF THE WORLD

By Jenna Myers

AV² provides enriched content that supplements and complements this book. Weigl's AV² books strive to create inspired learning and engage young minds in a total learning experience.

Your AV² Media Enhanced books come alive with...

Audio
Listen to sections of the book read aloud.

Key Words
Study vocabulary, and complete a matching word activity.

Go to **www.av2books.com**, and enter this book's unique code.

Video
Watch informative video clips.

Quizzes
Test your knowledge.

BOOK CODE

Q738335

Embedded Weblinks
Gain additional information for research.

Slide Show
View images and captions, and prepare a presentation.

AV² by Weigl brings you media enhanced books that support active learning.

Try This!
Complete activities and hands-on experiments.

... and much, much more!

Published by AV² by Weigl
350 5th Avenue, 59th Floor
New York, NY 10118

Websites: www.av2books.com www.weigl.com

Library of Congress Cataloging-in-Publication Data
Myers, Jenna.
 The J. Paul Getty Museum / Jenna Myers.
   pages cm. -- (Museums of the world)
 ISBN 978-1-4896-3256-2 (hardcover : alk. paper) -- ISBN 978-1-4896-3257-9 (softcover : alk. paper) -- ISBN 978-1-4896-3258-6 (single-user ebk.)
-- ISBN 978-1-4896-3259-3 (multi-user ebk.)1. J. Paul Getty Museum--Juvenile literature. 2. Art museums-
-California--Los Angeles--Juvenile literature. 3. Los Angeles (Calif.)--Buildings, structures, etc.--Juvenile
literature. I. Title.

N582.M25M94 2014
708.194'94--dc23
                    2014038742

Printed in Brainerd, Minnesota, in the United States of America
1 2 3 4 5 6 7 8 9 0 18 17 16 15 14

122014
WEP051214

Editor: Heather Kissock
Designer: Dean Pickup

Every reasonable effort has been made to trace ownership and to obtain permission to reprint copyright material. The publishers would be pleased to have any errors or omissions brought to their attention so that they may be corrected in subsequent printings.

Weigl acknowledges Getty Images, Alamy, Corbis, iStock, Newscom, and the J. Paul Getty Museum as its primary image suppliers for this title.

Contents

What Is the Getty Museum?

The J. Paul Getty Museum, often called the Getty Museum, is situated in Los Angeles, California. It is known as one of the most informative art museums in the world. This museum is incredibly popular not only because of its extensive art collection, but also because it is surrounded by stunning scenery. The Getty Center, the massive complex that houses the Getty Museum, overlooks downtown Los Angeles, the Pacific Ocean, and the mountains in Santa Monica.

The doors to the Getty Museum opened to the public in 1954. Ever since its first year, the museum has inspired curiosity, enjoyment, and understanding of the **visual arts**. It does this by collecting, **conserving**, and **exhibiting** works of art of exceptional quality and historical importance. The **collections** found in the Getty Museum feature artwork dating from ancient times through to the 21st century and take visitors on a historical journey through Europe, Asia, and the United States. The Getty Museum attracts people from Los Angeles and around the world, who visit the museum to enjoy and study art in an inspiring and interesting setting.

The Getty Museum's collections contain

65,104 separate objects.

With more than

1 million visitors per year, the Getty is one **of the most visited** museums in the United States.

An electric tram takes visitors up the hill to the Getty Center. The ride takes **5 minutes.**

Admission to the Getty Museum is FREE.

The Getty Center is an institution dedicated to the visual arts. The J. Paul Getty Museum plays a key role in the center's operations.

History of the Getty Museum

The Getty Museum is named after its founder, Jean Paul Getty, who strongly believed in making art available to the public. He decided to open his own museum to provide public access to his personal collection of artwork, which included Greek and Roman **antiquities**, 18th-century French furniture, and European paintings. As the collection expanded, it soon outgrew the museum space. Getty made plans to build a new museum in Malibu, California, called the Getty Villa. He died two years after it opened. As part of his will, Getty left a large portion of his fortune to fund the J. Paul Getty Museum. The people in charge of the museum's inheritance, the J. Paul Getty Trust, used some of this money to construct the Getty Center in Los Angeles.

Over time, the Getty collection grew to include sculptures, some of which reflect ancient people and ancient times.

1953 Jean Paul Getty establishes the J. Paul Getty Trust and J. Paul Getty Museum.

1970 Construction begins on the Getty Villa.

| 1950 | 1960 | 1965 | 1970 |

1954 The J. Paul Getty Museum opens in Getty's ranch house in Malibu.

1968 Getty conceives and plans a new museum called the Getty Villa.

The Getty Villa is modeled after a Roman country house that was built in the city of Herculaneum in the 1st century AD.

1974 The recently constructed Getty Villa opens as the new home of the J. Paul Getty Museum.

1984 Construction of the Getty Center begins.

2006 The Getty Villa is re-opened.

1975   **1980**   **1990**   **2010**

1976 J. Paul Getty dies on June 6 at the age of 83.

1982 On February 28, the J. Paul Getty Museum receives the money it inherited from J. Paul Getty. It totals about $1.2 billion.

1997 The Getty Villa closes for renovations, while the Getty Center, and its museum, open to the public.

Key People

The development of the J. Paul Getty Museum began with just one man. However, there were other key people who were instrumental in getting the Getty Museum established, operating, and serving a varied audience. Some of these people contributed by designing the structures that house the museum. Others played a key role in developing the collections and programs that have made the museum world-renowned.

Jean Paul Getty (1892–1976)

Jean Paul Getty was born on December 15, 1892, in Minneapolis, Minnesota. After graduating from England's Oxford University in 1914, Getty began working with his father in the family's oil company. He became president of the company in 1930. Under his leadership, Getty Oil became one of the largest oil companies in the world. The wealth Getty accumulated from the business allowed him to begin collecting art. Getty remained president of Getty Oil until his death of heart failure in 1976.

J. Paul Getty was a millionaire by the time he was 24 years old.

Richard Meier (1934–Present)

The Getty Center, and the museum inside, were designed by American architect Richard Meier. Born in Newark, New Jersey, on October 12, 1934, Meier graduated from Cornell University with a degree in **architecture**. He was soon working at Skidmore, Owings, & Merrill (SOM), one of the country's best-known architectural firms. In 1963, Meier formed his own company. By the mid-1970s, he was designing buildings for countries all over the world. He quickly earned a reputation for designing white buildings with strong geometric shapes.

In 1984, one year before starting work on the Getty Center, Richard Meier won the prestigious Pritzker Architecture Prize.

Harold M. Williams (1928–Present)

In 1981, the Getty's Board of Trustees chose Harold
M. Williams to become the founding president and
Chief Executive Officer (CEO) of the J. Paul Getty
Trust. Williams brought a wealth of experience
to the job. A graduate of Harvard Law School,
Williams was the chairman of the U.S. Securities and
Exchange Commission and a professor and dean at
the University of California (Los Angeles) Graduate
School of Management. He was instrumental in
planning and developing the Getty Center's research
center and library, its conservation institute, and its
art history and arts education programs, along with its **grant**
program and a variety of other initiatives. Williams' dedication
to the arts and his tireless work to help create the modern
Getty was recognized in 2013 when he received the
J. Paul Getty Founder's Award.

Harold M. Williams served as the president of the J. Paul Getty Trust from 1981 to 1998.

Nancy Englander (1944–Present)

Nancy Englander played an integral role in the Getty Center's early years.
Hired in 1981 as the Getty's director of program planning
and analysis, Englander brought a wealth of experience
to the role. She had previously been the director of
museum programs at the National Endowment
for the **Humanities**. Working alongside Harold
M. Williams, Englander helped put together the
general structure for the Getty, creating a master
plan outlining its goals and the steps it would take
to reach them. Englander was also honored in 2013
with the J. Paul Getty Founder's Award.

Nancy Englander was considered the second-in-command, after Williams, during the development of the Getty Center.

The Getty Museum Today

Jean Paul Getty believed that art could play an important role in a person's life and that art could be for enjoyment while also serving an educational purpose. The Getty Museum continues to advance these beliefs in its collections, exhibitions, and programming. The museum offers visitors a broad range of art to view, including paintings, drawings, **illuminated manuscripts**, sculptures, **decorative arts**, and photographs. The museum is also continually working to acquire new masterpieces and create exhibits that help people see art in a new light. The Getty Museum has contributed greatly to the reputation of the Getty Center as a whole, helping it to gain respect around the world for its commitment to the visual arts and humanities.

The museum's entrance hall is circular, with glass walls to let in natural light.

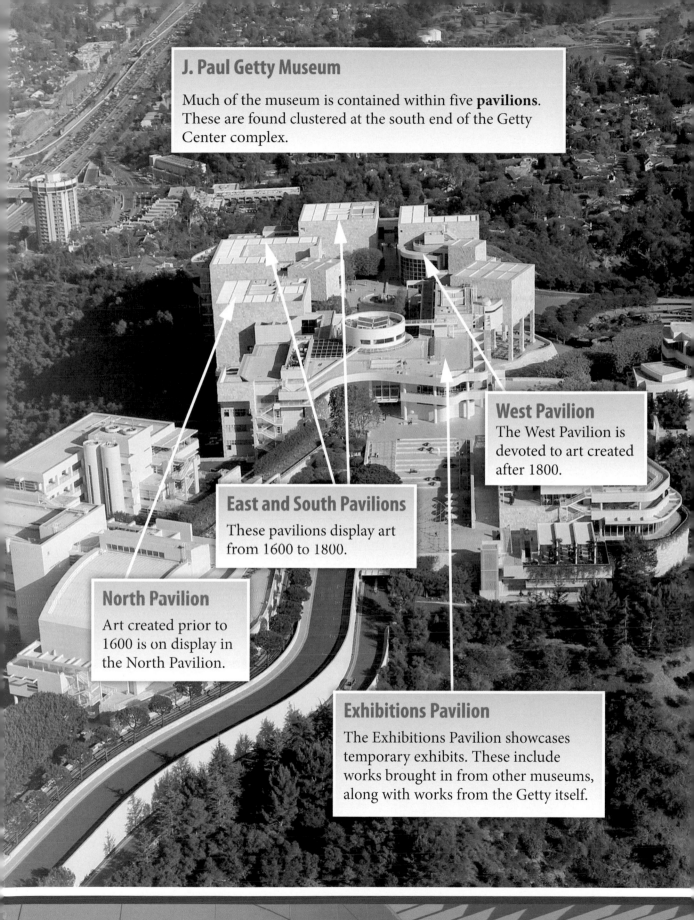

J. Paul Getty Museum

Much of the museum is contained within five **pavilions**. These are found clustered at the south end of the Getty Center complex.

West Pavilion
The West Pavilion is devoted to art created after 1800.

East and South Pavilions
These pavilions display art from 1600 to 1800.

North Pavilion
Art created prior to 1600 is on display in the North Pavilion.

Exhibitions Pavilion
The Exhibitions Pavilion showcases temporary exhibits. These include works brought in from other museums, along with works from the Getty itself.

Touring the Getty Museum

The Getty Museum's two locations contrast each other in appearance. The modern Los Angeles pavilions surround a central courtyard and are connected by glass walkways and open terraces. The Getty Villa's architecture reflects the buildings of ancient Rome. The art within both, however, extends across centuries.

North Pavilion Art from the **Middle Ages** and the **Renaissance** is on display in the North Pavilion. The upper level features paintings created prior to 1600. Sculptures and decorative art are found on the lower level. The museum's collection of illuminated manuscripts are also on display in this pavilion.

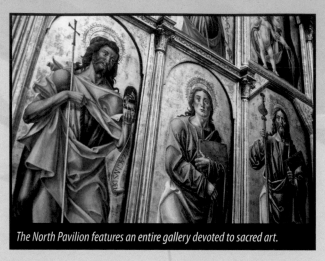

The North Pavilion features an entire gallery devoted to sacred art.

The art of the East Pavilion extends outdoors, decorating the outer walls of the building.

East and South Pavilions These two pavilions represent two centuries of art. European paintings from the 17th century are found in the East Pavilion, while the South Pavilion focuses on 18th-century works. Paintings are on the upper levels, and decorative arts are below. The lower level of the East Pavilion also contains sculptures dating from 1600 to 1800.

West Pavilion The West Pavilion houses 19th-century paintings, as well as sculptures and Italian decorative arts from the 18th and 19th centuries. It is also home to the Center for Photographs, which provides rotating displays of the museum's photography collection.

Like all of the museum's galleries, artwork in the West Pavilion is organized by era and artist nationality.

Getty Villa The Getty Museum's antiquities collection is housed at the Getty Villa. The villa's 28 galleries showcase the art and **artifacts** of the ancient Greeks, Romans, and Etruscans. Some of the objects on display date back to 6500 BC.

More than 1,200 antiquities are on display in the Villa at any time.

The Getty Center's research library holds more than **1 million** reference volumes.

Approximately **44,000** antiquities are kept at the Getty Villa.

In 2014, *Time Magazine* named the Getty one of the **top 25 museums in the world.**

The Getty has **58,000** square feet of exhibit space. (5,388 square meters)

30 The number of sculptures found on the museum's grounds

16% of the art on display in the museum was **personally collected** by Jean Paul Getty.

The Getty's **photography** collection includes more than **60,000** images.

The **14 galleries** of decorative arts form their own **mini-museum**.

The museum's collection of **illuminated** manuscripts represent nearly every region of **Europe**.

$ $ $ $ $ $ $ $

Irises is one of the most expensive paintings to ever be sold, costing an owner **$53.9 million** in 1987.

Treasures of the Getty Museum

The Getty Museum houses one of the country's most important collections of European art. Paintings by masters such as Monet and van Gogh encourage an appreciation of art in all its forms. Decorative arts and other artifacts give visitors insight into different times and places. Modern art sculptures stimulate thought and discussion. Together, the collection fulfills J. Paul Getty's wish to educate through art.

On display at the Getty are 308 paintings, 727 sculptures and decorative art objects, and a large collection of photographs, drawings, and manuscripts.

Irises has often been compared to the style of painting found on Japanese woodblocks of the 17th century.

Irises Painted the year before his death in 1890, *Irises* is one of Vincent van Gogh's most celebrated paintings. Van Gogh never intended it to be a masterpiece, however. It was simply a study of some flowers he saw in a garden in France. For this reason, there are no sketches or drawings of the work, only the work itself.

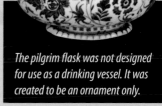

The pilgrim flask was not designed for use as a drinking vessel. It was created to be an ornament only.

Pilgrim Flask Made in Florence, Italy in the 1580s, this porcelain flask is an example of Europe's earliest porcelain. The flask was created in the Medici Porcelain Manufactory, which strived to create porcelain similar in quality to that of China. It is one of only about 60 Medici porcelain pieces left in the world.

Sunrise (Marine) shows the harbor of Le Havre, an industrial port on the coast of France.

Sunrise (Marine) Claude Monet's *Sunrise (Marine)* is studied by scholars around the world. Painted in 1873, it is well-known as an example of Monet's *plein air*, or "outdoor," approach to painting. This was one of the first paintings Monet created in the **Impressionist** style that would later lead him to his greatest success.

Bronze Form Found on the grounds of the Getty Center, Henry Moore's *Bronze Form* is more than 14 feet (4.3 meters) tall and weighs 4,200 pounds (1,905 kilograms). This huge bronze sculpture is often compared to an upright human figure. It was completed in 1985, only one year before Moore's death.

Henry Moore's Bronze Form is one of the first works of art to greet visitors to the Getty Center.

Collection Conservation

Conservation is an important part of almost all of the activities at the Getty Museum. In fact, the Getty has four conservation departments that each focus on a specific area of specialty. These areas are antiquities, decorative arts and sculpture, paintings, and paper. The Getty has about 25 conservators and support staff who perform a wide range of services for the museum. These professionals support the Getty's effort to exhibit and explain the collections, and to preserve them for the enjoyment and education of future generations.

A Controlled Environment Humidity and temperature can both cause problems for the works of art if not maintained properly. The Getty has installed climate control technologies within its galleries to ensure that works receive no more heat or moisture than they need. Fans and filters also benefit the collections by improving ventilation and air circulation throughout the building.

Paintings can crack and flake if they are exposed to changing humidity levels.

Cleaning The task of cleaning a work of art often involves removing dirt and grime from its surface. It can also involve removing layers of paint from previous **restoration** attempts. Conservators at the Getty Museum use cleaning agents that act on one layer of the work without affecting the layer being preserved. The conservators take care not to leave any harmful residue on the work of art after it has been cleaned.

Cleaning works of art is a delicate and meticulous process. Conservators must ensure that the correct tools and techniques are being used to avoid damaging the art.

The Getty's conservators are in demand around the world. They have traveled to various countries, including Egypt, to help create conservation plans for historically important works of art.

Surface Judgment

Before a work of art can be restored, the Getty's conservators have to assess the work's condition. Polynomial texture mapping (PTM) is a technique that enables conservators to look at the surface of an object under different lighting conditions. The technique allows conservators to assess surface changes caused by previous conservation or natural aging and plan an appropriate course of treatment.

Studying the surface of a painting provides conservators with insight into the materials and techniques used to create the art. This helps them plan a conservation program for the work.

Assessing Light

Art galleries must ensure that artworks are displayed in light that will not cause them damage. Getty conservation staff use microfadeometers to study how quickly colors on an artwork change when exposed to light. These tools use a tiny spot of very intense light as a probe to measure color changes in artworks that are sensitive to light exposure. The results help conservators determine the lighting required for specific artworks.

Conservators often rotate artwork so that pieces are not kept in light for extended periods of time. This helps prevent fading or color changes.

The Getty Museum in the World

The Getty Museum is committed to educating the public about art. It runs a variety of events and programs that allow people of all ages to learn about and experience art and culture. In addition to the public programs at the museum, **outreach** programs are also offered. These programs bring information and services about the museum to people all over the world.

Education The Getty Museum and Getty Villa offer a wide range of courses and demonstrations about art and art appreciation. Some of these courses study the theory of art, delving into its history and studying artists from past eras. Other courses allow people to interact with different art forms and current artists. Participants can take classes relating to different **media** and learn techniques from practicing artists.

Digital guides located throughout the museum help visitors learn more about the works on display.

Publications The **curators** and conservators at the Getty are experts in their fields. The Center encourages them to share their knowledge through its publishing program. Every year, the museum produces a number of books written by Getty staff. Topics range from biographies of specific artists to overviews of conservation projects. These publications are sold in bookstores around the world.

Many of the books written by museum staff are sold in the Getty Museum's bookstore.

Traveling Exhibits

People in other parts of the world can see works from the Getty's collections without traveling to the United States. The Getty regularly sends exhibits to other museums to be displayed in their galleries. These exhibits are often arranged around a theme to help visitors understand the art in a specific **context**. The Getty also loans individual pieces from its collections to other museums when the piece will help support a planned exhibition.

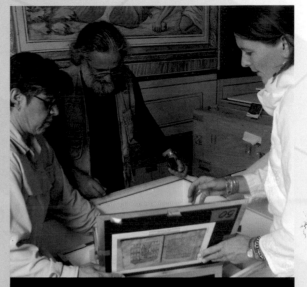

The Getty Museum also brings in exhibits from other museums and institutions. In 2006, the museum hosted a traveling exhibit from Egypt that featured religious icons from a monastery on Mount Sinai.

Online Community

Having a strong online presence helps the Getty reach out to an international audience. The museum is active on social media, sending out notices of exhibitions and upcoming events to followers. It also uses social media to further its goals of engaging and educating the public about art. Videos posted to the museum's YouTube channel provide viewers with behind-the-scenes tours of the museum and the Getty Center. The museum's own website features games for young art lovers.

Instructional videos are often uploaded to the Getty's YouTube channel. These videos show people how to produce their own art.

Looking to the Future

The Getty Museum is always looking for ways to show people the vital role that art plays in their lives. One way the Getty showcases the value of art is through its foundation. The Getty Foundation supports people and institutions committed to advancing a greater understanding and preservation of the visual arts in Los Angeles and around the world. In 2014, the foundation announced an initiative called Keeping It Modern, which will focus on giving grants toward the conservation of some of the world's most iconic 20th-century buildings.

The museum continues to expand its collections and develop new educational programs for its visitors. In 2014 alone, the museum acquired works by several master artists, including sculptor Auguste Rodin and painters Édouard Manet and Georges Seurat. The museum is committed to growing its collection, and in doing so, providing its visitors with new insight into a variety of art forms.

While the Getty Museum already has two paintings by Manet, Portrait of Julien de la Rochenoire is its first pastel by the artist. The portrait is on display in the museum's West Pavilion.

Australia's Sydney Opera House is one of the 10 buildings to receive a conservation grant under the Keeping It Modern program.

Activity

Each of the Getty Museum's pavilions displays artwork that has been arranged by some kind of theme. Arranging art by theme helps visitors understand it better. They can view a number of works that are linked to each other in a concrete way. Curators put great effort into developing themes for their art exhibitions.

Imagine that you are working as a curator in one of the Getty Museum's five pavilions. Go to the Getty Museum's website, and find the objects that are found within this pavilion. Study the objects found in one of the pavilion's galleries closely.

Answer the following questions about the objects located in the gallery you chose.

1. What is the theme that ties all of the objects together?

2. Why do you think these objects were chosen for the exhibit?

3. Would you display the objects differently? Why or why not?

4. What are the names of some of the artists who have work housed in this gallery?

5. What is your favorite piece of art in this gallery? Why do you like it best?

Getty Museum Quiz

1 Where is the Getty Museum located?

2 Who is the Getty Museum named after?

3 When did the Getty Center open to the public?

4 What kind of art is on display at the Getty Villa?

5 Who painted *Irises*?

ANSWERS:

1. Los Angeles, California **2.** Jean Paul Getty **3.** 1997
4. Antiquities **5.** Vincent van Gogh

Key Words

antiquities: objects from ancient times

architecture: the design of buildings and other structures

artifacts: objects that were made by people in the past

collections: art and artifacts collected for exhibit and study in a museum, and kept as part of its holdings

conserving: protecting objects from deterioration

context: the setting of a word or event

curators: people who manage, study, and care for a museum collection

decorative arts: high-quality objects that are both useful and beautiful

exhibiting: displaying objects or artwork within a theme

grant: money given to people or institutions to be used for a particular purpose

humanities: areas of study that relate to human life and ideas

illuminated manuscripts: documents that are decorated with gold or colored designs and pictures

Impressionist: a style of painting developed in France in the 1870s

media: specific types of artistic techniques

Middle Ages: the period of time associated with the 12th to 15th centuries

outreach: the process of bringing information or services to people

pavilions: buildings connected to larger buildings

Renaissance: a period between 1500 AD and 1800 AD

restoration: the act or process of returning something to its original condition by repairing it, cleaning it, etc.

visual arts: creations that people can look at, such as a drawing or painting

Index

Log on to www.av2books.com

AV² by Weigl brings you media enhanced books that support active learning. Go to www.av2books.com, and enter the special code found on page 2 of this book. You will gain access to enriched and enhanced content that supplements and complements this book. Content includes video, audio, weblinks, quizzes, a slide show, and activities.

AV² Online Navigation

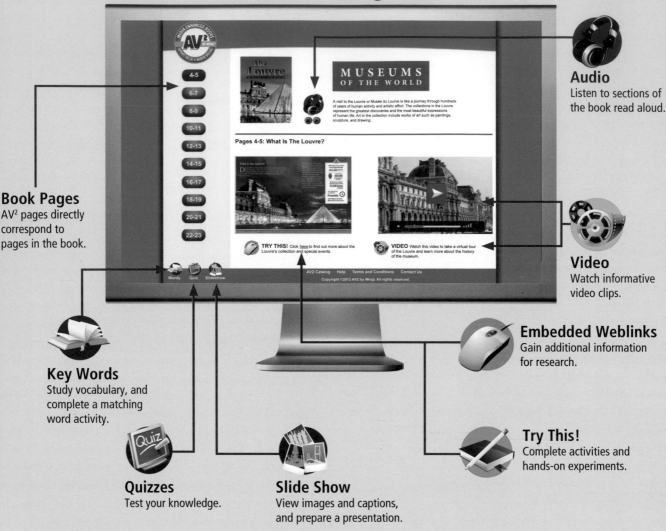

Book Pages
AV² pages directly correspond to pages in the book.

Key Words
Study vocabulary, and complete a matching word activity.

Quizzes
Test your knowledge.

Slide Show
View images and captions, and prepare a presentation.

Audio
Listen to sections of the book read aloud.

Video
Watch informative video clips.

Embedded Weblinks
Gain additional information for research.

Try This!
Complete activities and hands-on experiments.

AV² was built to bridge the gap between print and digital. We encourage you to tell us what you like and what you want to see in the future.

Sign up to be an AV² Ambassador at www.av2books.com/ambassador.

Due to the dynamic nature of the Internet, some of the URLs and activities provided as part of AV² by Weigl may have changed or ceased to exist. AV² by Weigl accepts no responsibility for any such changes. All media enhanced books are regularly monitored to update addresses and sites in a timely manner. Contact AV² by Weigl at 1-866-649-3445 or av2books@weigl.com with any questions, comments, or feedback.